The Bat and the Crocodile

AN ABORIGINAL STORY
Told by Jacko Dolumyu and Hector Jandany
Compiled by Pamela Lofts

SCHOLASTIC
SYDNEY AUCKLAND NEW YORK TORONTO LONDON MEXICO CITY
NEW DELHI HONG KONG BUENOS AIRES PUERTO RICO

This is the story the old people told us about Bat and Crocodile.

It's from the Dreamtime.

There was a lizard . . .
and he was hungry!
He thought Crocodile would be good tucker.

Lizard wanted Crocodile killed
so he could eat him.
He wanted Bat to kill Crocodile.

'Hey Bat,' he said, 'that Crocodile
reckons you smell awful.
He doesn't want you coming round
the corroboree tonight.'

'Ah well,' said Bat, 'if I'm too smelly I'll just have to go back to camp.'

Crocodile was dancing away
and shaking his shoulders.
'Move closer to the fire,' said Bat.
'I can't see you.'

But Bat really wanted to see that corroboree.
He went back to camp and
picked up his spear and woomera.

When Bat came back to the corroboree,
everyone was singing away.

Old Crocodile came out
all decorated and painted up.

'Build the fire to light up the place,' said Bat.
'I want Crocodile to dance close to the fire
so I can see him better.'

Bat moved back into the shadows
and started to hook up
his spear to his woomera.

Suddenly, Bat threw his spear
from that dark place.

It speared Crocodile right through the heart
and killed him.

'He speared him, he speared him.
Poor Crocodile,' shouted everybody.

They were really wild with Bat
and started to chase him.
Bat went for his life up into the hills . . .

. . . and escaped into a cave.

Everybody poked their spears
through holes at the front of the cave,
trying to get Bat.

But Bat thought of a trick.
He cut his tongue and put blood
on each one of those pointy spears.

Then he pretended to gasp for air.
Everyone was outside listening.

'We got him!' they said.
'Look, there is blood on the spears.
He's dead!'

And they all cheered and headed back to camp.

When they had gone a little way,
Bat popped up from the cave
and started singing:

'Who are you going to kill,
who are you going to kill?
Who's the tricky one,
who's the tricky one?'

'Look, he's still alive,' they said.
Everyone rushed back up the hill
with their spears.

But that tricky Bat
jumped into the cave again.

He put more blood
on those spears poking through
and pretended to gasp for air.

They looked at their spears again.
'There's a lot of blood here!
He must be dead now!' they said.
'Let's go.'

Bat watched them.
He waited until they were far away.
Then he jumped out of the cave
and sang his song again.

They started to come back again
and he disappeared into the cave.

It went on and on like that
until Bat won the game.
'He's too clever for us,' they said,
and left him alone.

Bat is still up there
in that cave where they left him.
He lives there forever.

You can still see the holes in that cave
where the spears poked through.